A Lifestyle of

Unceasing Prayer

9 Scriptural Tips for a Constant Prayer
Life that Brings Results

Nikeiza McJoy

Copyright © 2022 by Nikeiza McJoy.

All rights reserved. No part of this book may be reproduced, or stored in a retrieval system, or transmitted in any form or by any means, electronic, mechanical, photocopying, recording, or otherwise, without express written permission of the author.

Disclaimer

The recommendations in this material might not be appropriate for everyone. The information in this book is distributed on an "as is" basis, without warranty. Although every precaution has been taken in the preparation of this material the author shall have no liability to any person or entity with respect to any loss or damage caused or alleged to be caused directly or indirectly by the information contained in this book.

Scripture is taken from the;

King James Version (KJV)

New King James Version (NKJV)

New International Version (NIV)

Good News Translation (GNT)

English Standard Version (ESV)

Foreword

As Christians, we are called to a commitment of constant prayer (Matthew 26: 41a). Many may have inner doubts about prayer, wondering why our prayers never seem to be answered, or wondering just how we can constantly be in prayer as the Lord advised. This little book is a compilation of tips on how to stay in constant and effective prayer. The Lord has taught me these tips through the years via personal experiences, preaching ceremonies heard, and pieces of advice from others. The book is written as a quick guide that one can grab and go through whenever they need a spiritual lift. It can be used as often as needed.

Stay blessed as you make unceasing prayer your lifestyle.

Contents

Foreword vii

Chapter 1: Pray Without Ceasing 1

Preparing for Prayer 6

Chapter 2: Tip 1 - Have Faith in God 7

Chapter 3: Tip 2 - Forgive, and Ask for God's Forgiveness 9

The Active Prayer Session 15

Chapter 4: Tip 3 - Praise and Worship God 16

Chapter 5: Tip 4 - Offer your Prayers with a Grateful Heart 21

Chapter 6: Tip 5 - Invite the Holy Spirit to Help you Pray, and Use God's Word in Prayer 28

Chapter 7: Tip 6 - Believe that you Have Received what you are Praying for and Do Not Doubt 36

After the Prayer Session 40

Chapter 8: Tip 7 - Stay Obedient to God 41

Chapter 9: Tip 8 - Persist in Prayer 46

Chapter 10: Tip 9 - Be a Blessing to Others 51

Chapter 11: In a Nutshell 54

PRAYERS FOR DIVINE PROTECTION AND PROVISION. 56

Chapter 1: Pray Without Ceasing

Christians are called to a commitment of constant prayer. Jesus encouraged unceasing prayer. He talked about it on several occasions, as we see in a couple of examples below;

Then He spoke a parable to them, that men always ought to pray and not lose heart.

Luke 18:1 NKJV

"Watch and pray so that you will not fall into temptation."

Matthew 26:41a NIV

Apostle Paul gave a similar message to several audiences, as we see in a few examples below;

Rejoice always, pray without ceasing, in everything give thanks; for this is the will of God in Christ Jesus for you.

1 Thessalonians 5:16-18 NKJV

Rejoicing in hope, patient in tribulation, continuing steadfastly in prayer.

Romans 12:12 NKJV

Continue earnestly in prayer, being vigilant in it with thanksgiving;

Colossians 4:2 NKJV

So how do we stay in constant prayer?

How do we keep the fire burning in the midst of doubt?

How do we keep believing God's promise when everything seems to be going wrong?

Christianity is more about how we live than how we pray during a prayer session. We have to make the gospel a living reality, not a message we receive in church, and forget it the moment we get out.

The gospel is a guide to daily living!

Prayer should be our lifestyle. Prayer should not be a burden but a joy, a treasured moment with God our loving Father. We should be careful that our prayer pattern is not a boring and tiresome routine. The devil can trick us into a tedious prayer pattern to constantly nag us and lead us into boredom. Then we would later lose our zeal and eventually become spiritually weak.

But how do we pray unceasingly then? Where do we get the blueprint to follow?

From the Bible, we get pointers that the skill/art of prayer is taught. We know that at some point, the disciples of Jesus had to ask Him to teach them to pray.

Now it came to pass, as He was praying in a certain place, when He ceased, that one of His disciples said to Him, "Lord, teach us to pray, as John also taught his disciples."

So He said to them, "When you pray, say:

Our Father in heaven

Hallowed be Your name.

Your kingdom come.

Your will be done

On earth as it is in heaven.

Give us day by day our daily bread.

And forgive us our sins,

For we also forgive everyone who is indebted to us.

And do not lead us into temptation,

But deliver us from the evil one."

Luke 11:1-4 NKJV

We have to be taught to pray. We see from the passage we have just read that John taught his disciples to pray. Likewise, Jesus taught His disciples to pray. Jesus instantly responded to that request and started teaching them right away. He started by giving them the model prayer, the "Our Father". The Lesson did not end with the "Our Father" prayer. He continued to reveal key principles of prayer throughout that chapter and on many other occasions. We will extract these principles in the following chapters and draw lessons applicable to our daily life as we strive to make unceasing prayer our lifestyle.

This book quickly discusses tips for effective prayer, to add to the principles you already know and practice. These tips are for continuous prayer, a prayer manifested in the way we live, living to glorify God.

The tips are organized into three main sections; preparing for prayer, the active prayer session, and after the prayer session (or in-between prayer sessions, since prayer sessions will not end for a Christian).

Before we go to the tips, close your eyes and pray the following prayer points fervently.

1. *Lord Jesus, teach me to pray as you did with Your disciples in Jesus' name.*
2. *Holy Spirit, please open my eyes to the secrets of unceasing prayer in Jesus' name*

Praise the Lord!

Preparing for Prayer

Chapter 2: Tip 1 - Have Faith in God

Christian prayer is basically addressed to God. Even when a Christian is engaged in active spiritual warfare, it is by the authority of God that one engages in the warfare. That means, for one to pray, they have to;

- ✓ Believe in the existence of God,
- ✓ Acknowledge the omnipotence of God (His unlimited power and authority), and
- ✓ Trust in Him and be loyal to Him.

Foremost, prayer requires faith in God. The effectiveness of our prayer life depends on it. This faith should come from the realization that we need God, that we are nothing on our own, and that God alone can sustain us. We cannot please God if we do not have faith. We cannot pray effectively if we do not believe that He exists. We cannot pray effectively if we do not believe that He cares for us and He wants our good. The Bible assures us that God rewards those who truly seek Him.

And without faith it is impossible to please God, because anyone who comes to Him must believe that He exists and that He rewards those who earnestly seek Him.

Hebrews 11:6 NIV

We read about the faith of Abraham in scripture. Abraham obeyed God when He called him to leave his ancestral home and go to a different place as explained in the book of Genesis. He left by faith and went to dwell in a foreign land, believing in God's promise. He believed that what God said to him is true and the promise God made to him will surely come to pass. This faith is accounted to him for righteousness.

And he [Abraham] believed in the Lord, and He accounted it to him for righteousness.

Genesis 15:6 NKJV

We too need to make a commitment to trust in God and to believe in His promises. We need to have assurance and confidence in Him, relying on His faithfulness. It is a choice one has to make.

Chapter 3: Tip 2 - Forgive, and Ask for God's Forgiveness

Making mistakes and offending God and those around us is inevitable. But God requires us to strive for holiness. We are called to a life of repentance. We have to resolve to obey God's commandments. This requires the conversion of the heart, a determination to fully obey God at all times and stay in the state of grace.

The "Our Father" prayer shows us that our forgiveness by God is conditional.

And forgive us our sins, for we also forgive everyone who is indebted to us.

Luke 11:4a NKJV

We need to forgive ALL who offend us. Our forgiveness of others comes first, then we can ask God to forgive us our offenses.

Forgiveness is a decision we make, regardless of how we feel about our offenders. Our feelings many times will not agree with the decision to forgive. But we have to forgive because this is what God requires from us.

And whenever you stand praying, if you have anything against anyone, forgive him, that your Father in heaven may also forgive you your trespasses. But if you do not forgive, neither will your Father in heaven forgive your trespasses.

Mark11:25-26 NKJV

Please note here that forgiving others is not synonymous with reconciliation with them. In reconciliation there is forgiveness. However, reconciliation goes further and works to restore an estranged relationship. Thus, reconciliation requires the involvement and willingness of both parties. There are situations where reconciliation may not be possible. For instance, where one party is not willing. In those situations, we are still required to forgive the offender. Forgiveness is one-sided. We independently decide to let go and not hold on to that offense. Forgiveness entails releasing our offenders and not holding grudges against them. Forgiveness does not guarantee reconciliation. But as believers, we should also seek reconciliation as the Bible instructs us.

"Therefore if you bring your gift to the altar, and there remember that your brother has something against you, leave your gift there

before the altar, and go your way. First be reconciled to your brother, and then come and offer your gift."

Matthew 5:23-24 NKJV

If it is possible, as much as depends on you, live peaceably with all men.

Romans 12:18 NKJV

So, we should pursue reconciliation as well. If it works, praise God! If it doesn't, at least we tried, and thank God.

Once we decide to forgive, let's ask for God's grace to help us forgive without harboring grievances. Let's ask God to help us let go of the anger and the bitterness so that we can be at peace. Then let us trust in His help. This is a process. In some cases, we might find ourselves struggling for long to truly let go of the bitterness and be at peace. Do not worry. As long as we have decided to forgive and pursue peace while trusting in God's help, we can proceed in prayer. Sooner or later the bitterness will vanish.

We too offend others and God countless times. We now have to ask God to forgive us our own sins. We can use Psalm 51 as a guide to help us repent sincerely. The blood of Jesus is also available for us to apply for our cleansing.

"For this is my blood of the covenant, which is poured out for many for the forgiveness of sins."

Matthew 26:28 ESV

But if we walk in the light, as he is in the light, we have fellowship with one another, and the blood of Jesus his Son cleanses us from all sin.

1 John 1:7 ESV

True repentance comes from a "broken and contrite heart" (Psalm 51:17). Let us repent sincerely before God and strive not to go back to our vomit.

Forgiven by God, we can then confidently dwell in His presence, for He is delighted with the prayers of the righteous.

The sacrifice of the wicked is an abomination to the LORD, but the prayer of the upright is

His delight.

>Proverbs 15:8 NKJV

The Lord is near to all who call upon Him, to all who call upon Him in truth.

>Psalm 145:18 NKJV

Even if we fall into sin again, we shouldn't despair. Let us run to God for forgiveness with a sincere heart and He shall renew our strength. For it is written that God upholds us.

The steps of a good man are ordered by the Lord, and He delights in his way. Though he fall, he shall not be utterly cast down; for the Lord upholds him with His hand.

>Psalm 37:23-24 NKJV

The enemy will tell us that God is angry with us and will not accept us back. What the devil actually wants is to keep us out of God's mercy. Do not believe the enemy, rather, drive him crazy by trusting in the mercy of God!

For His anger is but for a moment, His favor

is for life; weeping may endure for a night, but joy comes in the morning.

Psalm 30:5 NKJV

God's mercy endures forever, thus says the Bible. No matter how deep we may think we have been in sin, God is ready to forgive us and give us another chance.

It is also important to forgive ourselves. Sometimes, we get too hard on ourselves. We hold on to the guilt we feel. The enemy can use that to steal our peace. Let us explicitly state that we forgive ourselves as well. Then let us explicitly release our feelings of guilt unto God. Ask Him to take the guilty feelings from us and replace them with His peace.

The Active Prayer Session

Chapter 4: Tip 3 - Praise and Worship God

After we have made a commitment to trust in God, forgiven our offenders, and repented of our own offenses, it's now time to boldly approach God's throne and actively offer our prayer(s). Here, we are discussing an active prayer session, where we intentionally engage with God in prayer. This is the prayer session alluded to in Mark 11:25a, "*And whenever you stand praying, ...*" Having set things right first, now we can stand in prayer.

We enter God's presence with praise. It's time to give God praise and to worship Him. We approach God with reverence. In praising God, we express our gratitude for His love and mercy on us. We thank Him for what He does and for what He is able to do, for we know His doings exceed our imaginations. This tip may be familiar as many Christian congregations begin prayer services with hot sessions of praise and worship.

Enter His gates with thanksgiving, and into His courts with praise. Be thankful to Him, and bless His name.

Psalm 100:4

During a prayer session, we can praise God with singing and dancing, if possible. We can also listen to good praise and worship songs as we give God center place in our life. We can praise Him by boldly proclaiming His goodness like the way David started his prayer session in 1 Chronicles 29.

Therefore David blessed the Lord before all the assembly, and David said: "Blessed are You, Lord God of Israel, our Father, forever and ever.

Yours, O Lord, is the greatness, the power and the glory, the victory and the majesty;

For all that is in heaven and in earth is Yours; Yours is the kingdom, O Lord, and You are exalted as head over all.

Both riches and honor come from You, and You reign over all. In Your hand is power and might; In Your hand it is to make great and to give strength to all.

Now therefore, our God, we thank You and praise Your glorious name."

1 Chronicles 29:10-13 NKJV

Worship is our expression of reverence for God. It comes from our core in relation to what God means to us individually. The worshipper surrenders themselves completely to God and adores Him for who He is. For Christians, our worship is to God alone, no one, and nothing else. God commands us in the first commandment to Worship Him exclusively.

"You shall have no other gods before Me."

Exodus 20:3 NKJV

Oh come, let us worship and bow down; Let us kneel before the Lord our Maker. For He is our God, and we are the people of His pasture, and the sheep of His hand.

Psalm 95:6-7 NKJV

God is Spirit, and those who worship Him must worship in spirit and truth.

John 4:24 NKJV

Let us take a peep into how worship is done in heaven.

The four living creatures, each having six wings, were full of eyes around and within.

And they do not rest day or night, saying:

"Holy, holy, holy, Lord God Almighty, who was and is and is to come!"

Whenever the living creatures give glory and honor and thanks to Him who sits on the throne, who lives forever and ever, the twenty-four elders fall down before Him who sits on the throne and worship Him who lives forever and ever, and cast their crowns before the throne, saying:

"You are worthy, O Lord, to receive glory and honor and power; For You created all things, and by Your will they exist and were created."

Revelation 4:8-11 NKJV

Worship puts focus on God. In worship we acknowledge that God is worthy and our unworthiness comes to light, so we bow down to Him.

Therefore let us be grateful for receiving a kingdom that cannot be shaken, and thus let us offer to God acceptable worship, with reverence and awe, for our God is a consuming fire.

Hebrews 12:28-29 ESV

Worship and praise are a lifestyle. They are not limited to the active prayer session.

I will bless the Lord at all times; His praise shall continually be in my mouth.

Psalm 34:1 NKJV

Whoever offers praise glorifies Me; and to him who orders his conduct aright I will show the salvation of God.

Psalm 50:23 NKJV

Let everything that has breath praise the Lord. Praise the Lord!

Psalm 150:6 NKJV

We have to strive for a life of continual worship and praise of God.

Chapter 5: Tip 4 - Offer Your Prayers with a Grateful Heart

Be anxious for nothing, but in everything by prayer and supplication, with thanksgiving, let your requests be made known to God.

And the peace of God, which surpasses all understanding, will guard your hearts and minds through Christ Jesus.

Philippians 4:6-7 NKJV

Our attitude towards prayer is important. Prayer is not some kind of magic with which to sway God in whatever direction we desire. In prayer, we acknowledge the omnipotence of God, we acknowledge that we are nothing without Him, and we accept that we are ready to submit to His will. So, if our will is not in agreement with the will of God, then we surrender our will for His.

When addressing God in prayer, we should do it with reverence, giving God all the respect He deserves. Our approach in a heart-to-heart talk with God cannot be the same approach in spiritual warfare, where we wrestle against spiritual forces of evil mentioned in Ephesians 6:12.

For we do not wrestle against flesh and blood, but against principalities, against powers, against the rulers of the darkness of this age, against spiritual hosts of wickedness in the heavenly places.

Ephesians 6:12

We present our requests to God with respect and with a heart of surrender. We do not demand from God or command Him to do anything. We humbly ask, and utterly submit to His will. On the other hand, in spiritual warfare, we use the authority God gave us (Luke 10:19) and engage the spiritual forces of evil in battle backed by God.

Behold, I give you the authority to trample on serpents and scorpions, and over all the power of the enemy, and nothing shall by any means hurt you.

Luke 10:19 NKJV

Christ explicitly states that the authority He has given us is over all the power of the enemy. So, in spiritual warfare, we can command those evil forces to bow to God's will concerning us, using the authority given to us. We cannot take the language and attitude we use when addressing the evil forces and use the same when addressing God. NO.

Our prayer should come from a place of trust, and not a place of anxiety. Prayer shows that we have trust in God and we believe that He will hear our prayer and intervene for our good. Then why be anxious about anything? Anxiety comes when we worry about our situations. Behind anxiety is fear. In so many instances in the Bible, God tells us not to worry and not to fear. Worry and fear can cause more harm than whatever trouble we may be anticipating. God, in His Wisdom, tells us again and again not to worry, and not to fear. When experiencing uneasiness over some anticipated misfortune, what we are called to do as children of God, is to trust God, bring the issue to Him, and wait upon Him. God will give us peace. Let's take a look at several Bible verses on this issue.

Trust in the Lord with all your heart and lean not on your own understanding; in all your ways submit to him, and he will make your paths straight.

Proverbs 3:5-6 NIV

Cast your cares on the LORD and he will

sustain you; he will never let the righteous be shaken.

Psalm 55:22 NIV

Cast all your anxiety on him because he cares for you.

1 Peter 5:7 NIV

Whenever I am afraid, I will trust in you.

Psalm 56:3 NKJV

"Therefore do not worry about tomorrow, for tomorrow will worry about its own things. Sufficient for the day is its own trouble."

Matthew 6:34 NKJV

"Come to me, all you who are weary and burdened, and I will give you rest."

Matthew 11:28 NIV

"Peace I leave with you; my peace I give you. I do not give to you as the world gives. Do not let your hearts be troubled and do not be

afraid."

John 14:27 NIV

Let the peace of Christ rule in your hearts, since as members of one body you were called to peace. And be thankful.

Colossians 3:15 NIV

We even have "insurance cover" when we trust in God. See the insurance policy statement below;

Blessed is the man who trusts in the LORD, and whose hope is the LORD. For he shall be like a tree planted by the waters, which spreads out its roots by the river, and will not fear when heat comes; But its leaf will be green, and will not be anxious in the year of drought, nor will cease from yielding fruit.

Jeremiah 17:7-8 NKJV

Heat and drought will surely come, but when they do, we will be fully covered! And God continues to assure us about His goodwill towards us.

"For I know the plans I have for you," declares the Lord, "plans to prosper you and not to harm you, plans to give you hope and a future.

Then you will call on me and come and pray to me, and I will listen to you.

Jeremiah 29:11-12 NIV

As it has been revealed to us in scripture, let us trust in God and be at peace. The Lord will renew our strength as we wait upon Him.

But they that wait upon the Lord shall renew their strength; they shall mount up with wings as eagles; they shall run, and not be weary; and they shall walk, and not faint.

Isaiah 40:31 KJV

This is not passive waiting. God gives us strength as we seek him and as we rely on Him and not on our own strength. With renewed strength, we shall soar above all situations.

The comforting and encouraging verses we have seen are not saying that worry will not come. As long as we are in this world, things to worry us will come. But when that happens, let us quickly remember who we are in Christ, and what God calls us to do regarding the cares of this life. Let us embrace God's peace and actively close our hearts and minds to worry and fear.

This is the attitude we need to have when offering our prayers, no matter how grave our situation might be. Let us offer our prayers to God from a grateful heart, a heart that appreciates the privilege we have of being God's children. A heart that knows that God, as a Father, will not withhold anything good from us (Psalm 84:11). The joy of the Lord is our strength!

Chapter 6: Tip 5 - Invite the Holy Spirit to Help You Pray, and Use God's Word in Prayer

Now, with a thankful heart, in complete trust of God, we are ready to verbally offer our prayers. Prayer is basically addressed to God the Father, as we see in the "Our Father" prayer. We access the Father through Jesus, the Son.

Jesus said to him, "I am the way, and the truth, and the life. No one comes to the Father except through me."

John 14:6 ESV

Coming to the Father through Jesus is more than just adding "in the name of Jesus" at the end of our prayer. It is praying with the revelation of who Jesus is to us as the "way, the truth, and the life".

Jesus is the Word made flesh.

In the beginning was the Word, and the Word was with God, and the Word was God.

John 1:1 ESV

We need to know the Word of God, the Scripture. An encounter with the word of God is an encounter with Jesus. Then we will know the truth and the truth will set us free. The importance of daily Bible study, our daily spiritual bread, cannot be more emphasized. Christ Himself instructed us to abide by His word.

Then Jesus said to those Jews who believed Him, "If you abide in My word, you are My disciples indeed. And you shall know the truth, and the truth shall make you free."

John 8:31-32 NKJV

When Jesus prayed for His disciples in John chapter 17, He said the following;

"Sanctify them by Your truth. Your word is truth."

John 17:17 NKJV

It is in the word of God that the truth is revealed to us. By that truth, we are set free. Through the Word, we are cleansed.

In addition to being the way and the truth, we see that Jesus is life. The word of God is life.

But Simon Peter answered Him, "Lord, to whom shall we go? You have the words of eternal life."

John 6:68 NKJV

"Most assuredly, I say to you, the hour is coming, and now is, when the dead will hear the voice of the Son of God; and those who hear will live."

John 5:25 NKJV

So He humbled you, allowed you to hunger, and fed you with manna which you did not know nor did your fathers know, that He might make you know that man shall not live by bread alone; but man lives by every word that proceeds from the mouth of the LORD.

Deuteronomy 8:3 NKJV

So, we pray through Jesus Christ, fully aware that in the word of God we find the way, the truth, and the life. With this realization, our prayers get to a higher level of potency and bring results with ease.

However, our human nature limits us sometimes. Knowing our limitations, Christ provided a helper to us, the Spirit of truth.

"And I will pray the Father, and He will give you another Helper, that He may abide with you forever; the Spirit of truth, whom the world cannot receive, because it neither sees Him nor knows Him; but you know Him, for He dwells with you and will be in you".

John 14:16-17 NKJV

Likewise, the Spirit helps us in our weakness. For we do not know what to pray for as we ought, but the Spirit himself intercedes for us with groanings too deep for words.

Romans 8:26 ESV

Now we are set to offer our prayers to the Father, through Christ. But as we know that we are limited on our own, we invite the Holy Spirit to help us pray. Explicitly invite the Holy Spirit to help you pray. Praying through Christ, with the guidance of the Holy Spirit, will safeguard our prayers from being amiss. The book of James reveals to us that it is very possible to pray amiss.

You ask and do not receive, because you ask amiss, that you may spend it on your pleasures.

James 4:3 NKJV

The New International Version puts it this way;

When you ask, you do not receive, because you ask with wrong motives, that you may spend what you get on your pleasures.

James 4:3 NIV

We see here that our motive behind our request matters. Many times we pray amiss, motivated by our selfish desires. Both our desires and the motives behind those desires should be in alignment with God's will. Again, we see the important role of the word of God. In Scripture, we find the will of God for us His children, and the promises of God to us His Children. When we understand what God expects from us, we will pray in line with His will. And a prayer in line with God's will is effective.

Our prayer should be rooted in scripture. When we understand God's promises to us, we will confidently know whether our situation is God's will for us or not. If the situation is not God's will, we will confidently approach the throne of God in prayer. If the situation requires us to go on the battlefield, we will go into spiritual warfare with confidence. We will intervene in the spirit realm to bring about a turnaround to our situation. We will confidently use prayer to force what is happening in the physical realm to change and come into alignment with God's divine will and purpose for us.

Praying with scripture will also help us avoid using vain words as the Lord warned us;

But when ye pray, use not vain repetitions, as the heathen do: for they think that they shall be heard for their much speaking. Be not ye therefore like unto them: for your Father knoweth what things ye have need of, before ye ask him.

Matthew 6:7-8 KJV

Let's see the same verse in other versions.

And when you pray, do not keep on babbling like pagans, for they think they will be heard because of their many words. Do not be like them, for your Father knows what you need before you ask him.

Matthew 6:7-8 NIV

And when you pray, do not heap up empty phrases as the Gentiles do, for they think that they will be heard for their many words. Do not be like them, for your Father knows what you need before you ask him.

Matthew 6:7 ESV

Important to note here is that Jesus is teaching against the use of **"vain repetitions", "babbling"** and, **"empty phrases".**

When we pray using the word of God and guided by the Holy Spirit, our prayer will not be silly babbling. The words we use will not be vain repetitions but God's own powerful weapon revealed in Hebrews 4:12.

For the word of God is living and powerful, and sharper than any two-edged sword, piercing even to the division of soul and spirit, and of joints and marrow, and is a discerner of the thoughts and intents of the heart.

Hebrews 4:12 NKJV

So shall My word be that goes forth from My mouth; It shall not return to Me void, But it shall accomplish what I please, and it shall prosper in the thing for which I sent it.

Isaiah 55:11 NKJV

As Jesus tells us in Matthew 6:8, our Father already knows what we need before we even ask Him. We use prayer to cooperate with God in bringing to pass His will in our life. So, we apply the word that comes from God's mouth, the living and powerful weapon that's sharper than a two-edged sword, sending it forth to accomplish what God pleases, so that God's purpose prospers in our lives.

Chapter 7: Tip 6 - Believe That You Have Received What You are Praying for and Do Not Doubt

Christ revealed this to us when He cursed the fig tree. He told us that we should believe that we have received what we are praying for and we should not give doubt a chance.

*Therefore I say to you, whatever things you ask **when** you pray, believe that you receive them, and you will have them.*

Mark 11:24 NKJV (Emphasis added)

Notice that this version of the Bible says **"when"** you pray. The belief that you have received your request should be active even as you offer the prayer. As you are praying, you should believe in your heart that God will grant your request. We see this principle at work in the woman with the flow of blood, who touched the hem of Jesus' garment, in Mark chapter 5. Let's read it;

Now a certain woman had a flow of blood for twelve years, and had suffered many things from many physicians. She had spent all that she had and was no better, but rather grew worse. When she heard about Jesus, she came behind Him in the crowd and touched His garment. For she said, "If only I may touch His clothes, I shall be made well."

Immediately the fountain of her blood was dried up, and she felt in her body that she was healed of the affliction. And Jesus, immediately knowing in Himself that power had gone out of Him, turned around in the crowd and said, "Who touched My clothes?"

But His disciples said to Him, "You see the multitude thronging You, and You say, 'Who touched Me?'"

And He looked around to see her who had done this thing. But the woman, fearing and trembling, knowing what had happened to her, came and fell down before Him and told Him the whole truth. And He said to her, "Daughter, your faith has made you well. Go in peace, and be healed of your affliction."

Mark 5:25:34 NKJV

Matthew writes in chapter 9 verse 21, *For she said to herself, "If only I may touch His garment, I shall be made well."*

"She said to herself"

This was her inner belief. She strongly believed it. With her belief, she pressed on in the crowd until she was able to touch just the hem of the Master's garment. And what happened?

"Immediately the fountain of her blood was dried up, and she felt in her body that she was healed of the affliction."

Did Jesus rebuke her for her bold faith in action? On the contrary! Our Lord addressed her as "daughter" and complimented her faith! A person with this kind of faith is very close to the heart of Jesus. Such a person is not just any person or any woman, but a daughter/son. We see another instance of a display of strong faith that provoked Jesus to use this term of endearment again, in Mark 2:5, *when Jesus saw their faith, He said to the paralytic, "Son, your sins are forgiven you."*

May we get to higher levels of faith in Jesus' name.

After we have presented our requests to God, let us cultivate the habit of remaining silent for a while before God (5 minutes, maybe 10, it's up to us), to hear what He has to say.

"My sheep hear my voice, and I know them, and they follow me."

John 10:27 NKJV

While they were worshiping the Lord and fasting, the Holy Spirit said, "Set apart for me Barnabas and Saul for the work to which I have called them."

Acts 13:2 NIV

When we hear what He has to say, let's proceed to do as He instructs. If we don't hear anything at first, do not worry. Let us keep that practice in our prayer sessions and sooner or later we will hear Him. Some of us may receive God's instructions later in dreams or visions, let us take heed.

Then thank God for answering our prayers and close our prayer session with high praises to God.

After the Prayer Session

Chapter 8: Tip 7 - Stay Obedient to God

We have prayed, now what? The moments outside active prayer sessions are the crucial ones. It is in these moments that we are actually living life (doing chores, working our regular job and/or side hustle, taking care of kids, volunteering in our community, and many other things we do in life). It is very rare to actively engage in sin during an active prayer session. But now that we have prayed and are up and about our business, temptations to sin glare at us everywhere we turn. Challenges to our Christian walk are everywhere. Kids step on our toes, our spouse does something and we react, our innocent hang out with friends turns into a gossip session, our work colleague does something and we are offended, we get invited to places we know we shouldn't be and we find ourselves confused, and the list goes on. This is the time when we are "living life". Is this life we are living glorifying God?

It is important to stay spiritually alert in these moments. Remember, the enemy diligently seeks opportunities to attack us and take us away from God's path.

Be sober, be vigilant; because your adversary the devil walks about like a roaring lion, seeking whom he may devour.

1 Peter 5:8 NKJV

All our days, let us take the responsibility to obey God; not as a way of earning His favor but as an act of our love for Him. Remember, we are made righteous by grace, not by deeds.

Being justified freely by His grace through the redemption that is in Christ Jesus.

Romans 3:24 NKJV

Now to the one who works, wages are not credited as a gift but as an obligation. However, to the one who does not work but trusts God who justifies the ungodly, their faith is credited as righteousness.

Romans 4:4-5 NIV

We are saved by grace through faith in Christ, not by our works. However, our deeds must show whom we serve, as our

Lord Jesus tells us.

"If you love Me, keep My commandments."

John14:15 NKJV

These are the moments we have to put into practice what the Word says. Our study of scripture will help us to know how to respond to various situations.

Do not merely listen to the word, and so deceive yourselves. Do what it says.

James 1:22 NIV

We will know with clarity, using the lenses of God's word, what is right and what is wrong. With the help of the Holy Spirit, we will be inspired and empowered to choose what is right, regardless of whether it's a popular decision or not.

As we go about living, let us believe that God is working on our situation even if things don't seem to be changing, they may even be worsening. Let's continue to be faithful to God and cheerfully go about our daily business. If you gave yourself a special prayer period or fasting period, carry on with your devotion to the end even if you get negative results on the way. For example, you are expecting a job and trusting God that the application you sent will be successful. You may even have been invited for interviews for the job. So, you embark on say, 21 days of prayer and fasting. And along the way, maybe on day 17 of your prayer and fasting program, you receive a regret regarding the job. Do not abort your fasting and prayer program. Carry on to the end as you initially purposed. You can switch from a prayer of request to thanksgiving, praise, and worship. Choose to praise and thank God even if you don't understand. Let God do as He pleases regarding your situation and don't let the negative report disturb you. So, focus on God. God will surprise you.

Let's stay spiritually alert and continue in praise. Meditate on scripture as you go about your day. It could be a particular verse that spoke to your situation sharply. Turn it into a prayer point and keep praying it in your heart as you go about your busy day. This will help you to stay spiritually alert and offer continuous praises unto God. Praising God is more of our attitude in life than just something we do during prayer sessions. If we diligently study the Bible, the Holy Spirit will be dropping verses in our hearts and minds timely the moment we need them. But if we don't study the Bible, and in our memory, there are no files containing scripture, what will the Holy Spirit, our helper, use to guide and counsel us?

Your ears shall hear a word behind you, saying, "This is the way, walk in it," Whenever you turn to the right hand or whenever you turn to the left.

Isaiah 30:21 NKJV

Let our lives glorify God by purposefully living by His principles. Let us keep believing in God's love even amidst our problems. No matter what we go through, we know God is in control and we have to believe this and not doubt. Wherever we are and with whomever we are, let us stay obedient to our Master.

Chapter 9: Tip 8 - Persist in Prayer

Oftentimes, we realize that the situations we present to God do not always get resolved immediately. We have to pray about some issues again and again, with persistence until the situation changes for the better. In the book of Luke chapter 11, after our Lord Jesus gave His disciples the "Our Father Prayer", the lesson on prayer did not end there. Immediately after that prayer, Jesus gave them the parable of the friend at midnight. Let's read it;

And He said to them, "Which of you shall have a friend, and go to him at midnight and say to him, 'Friend, lend me three loaves; for a friend of mine has come to me on his journey, and I have nothing to set before him'; and he will answer from within and say, 'Do not trouble me; the door is now shut, and my children are with me in bed; I cannot rise and give to you'? I say to you, though he will not rise and give to him because he is his friend, yet because of his persistence he will rise and give him as many as he needs.

Luke 11: 5-8 NKJV

He gave them another parable to hit the same point home, in Luke chapter 18.

Then He spoke a parable to them, that men always ought to pray and not lose heart, saying: "There was in a certain city a judge who did not fear God nor regard man. Now there was a widow in that city; and she came to him, saying, 'Get justice for me from my adversary.' And he would not for a while; but afterward he said within himself, 'Though I do not fear God nor regard man, yet because this widow troubles me I will avenge her, lest by her continual coming she weary me.'"

Then the Lord said, "Hear what the unjust judge said. And shall God not avenge His own elect who cry out day and night to Him, though He bears long with them? I tell you that He will avenge them speedily. Nevertheless, when the Son of Man comes, will He really find faith on the earth?"

Luke 18:1-8 NKJV

Need I say more? Let us persist in prayer. In Luke chapter 11, after the parable of the friend at midnight, Jesus tells His disciples to keep asking, seeking, and knocking, "For **everyone** who asks receives, and he who seeks finds, and to him who knocks it will be opened" (Luke 11: 10 NKJV, emphasis added).

No matter how many active prayer sessions it might take for our issue to get resolved, let us keep praying and trusting God. Observing a silent moment during prayer will help us to hear God's direction, whether He wants us to do something regarding our situation, or that we have prayed about that issue enough and it's time to direct our prayers to something else, etc. Whatever He tells us, let's obey.

The Lord is good to everyone who trusts in Him, so it is best for us to wait in patience – to wait for Him to save us – and it is best to learn this patience in our youth.

Lamentation 3:25-27, GNT

Trust in God and patiently wait for him to intervene. Know that He will intervene in His time not our time. Rest assured, God's time is the best!

We also have to learn to persevere. There are some things God allows us to pass through for a purpose.

Every test that you have experienced is the

kind that normally comes to people. But God keeps His promise, and He will not allow you to be tested beyond your power to remain firm; at the time you are put to the test, He will give you the strength to endure it and so provide you with a way out.

> 1 Corinthians 10:13 GNT

Remember that as Christians, we share Christ's life in full, suffering inclusive. And suffering allowed by God sanctifies.

If the world hates you, keep in mind that it hated me first.

> John 15:18 NIV

Trust that God, in His infinite wisdom will grant that which is beneficial to our soul and for His glory. If this means our request not being granted as we wanted, know that He grants that which is better though might not be to our liking. Let us pray for the grace to submit to God's will.

And we know that all things work together for good to those who love God, to those who

are the called according to His purpose.
>Romans 8:28 NKJV

If the going gets tough and we need someone to help in prayer, remember that God put us in a community with family and lots of friends. Find someone trustworthy who can assist. We can also consult our pastor.

"Again I say to you that if two of you agree on earth concerning anything that they ask, it will be done for them by My Father in heaven.
>Matthew 18:19 NKJV

Let us persist in prayer until God intervenes in our situation.

Chapter 10: Tip 9 - Be a Blessing to Others

A Christian is called to do good works and be a blessing to others.

For we are his workmanship, created in Christ Jesus for good works, which God prepared beforehand, that we should walk in them.

Ephesians 2:10 NKJV

"Give, and it will be given to you: good measure, pressed down, shaken together, and running over will be put into your bosom. For with the same measure that you use, it will be measured back to you."

Luke 6:38 NKJV

One area of giving that we may have not given a lot of attention to is the giving of prayer. One secret that gets our prayers answered speedily is to intercede or to pray for others. Let's see it at work in scripture;

And so it was, after the Lord had spoken these

words to Job, that the Lord said to Eliphaz the Temanite, "My wrath is aroused against you and your two friends, for you have not spoken of Me what is right, as My servant Job has. Now therefore, take for yourselves seven bulls and seven rams, go to My servant Job, and offer up for yourselves a burnt offering; and My servant Job shall pray for you. For I will accept him, lest I deal with you according to your folly; because you have not spoken of Me what is right, as My servant Job has."

So Eliphaz the Temanite and Bildad the Shuhite and Zophar the Naamathite went and did as the Lord commanded them; for the Lord had accepted Job. And the Lord restored Job's losses when he prayed for his friends. Indeed the Lord gave Job twice as much as he had before

Job 42:7-10 NKJV

There is a revelation in verse 8 and verse 10 of Job chapter 42. The Lord wanted Job to pray for his friends as we see in verse 8. Job's friends obeyed God's instructions and went to Job. Job prayed for them as God required. The Lord restored Job's losses **when he prayed for his friends.** There is power in interceding for others, as long as our intercession is in line with God's will. Spend some time crying out to God to intervene in someone's situation. Give your all in the intercession as if you don't have your own pressing needs. As you give in this way, God cannot fail to attend to your own needs. Make praying for others your habit.

Chapter 11: In a Nutshell

Tips for a life of unceasing prayer, where prayer goes beyond the active prayer session and becomes our lifestyle;

Preparing for Prayer

Tip 1: Have faith in God. It is impossible to please God without faith.

Tip 2: Live a life of repentance. Constantly ask God to forgive your sins. Remember that God requires us to forgive our offenders first.

The Active Prayer Session

Tip 3: Start the active prayer session by worshipping and praising God.

Tip 4: Offer your prayers with a grateful heart. Approach God with reverence and pray from a place of trust.

Tip 5: Remember the Holy Spirit is our helper. Invite Him to help you pray and pray with God's words. This approach will ensure that our prayers are in line with God's will.

Tip 6: Believe that you have received what you are praying for, and do not doubt. Also practice a moment of silence during your prayer session to hear from God.

After the Active Prayer Session (In-between Prayer Sessions)

Tip 7: Stay obedient to God and apply God's word in your daily situations to live a life that glorifies God. Regular Bible study is key.

Tip 8: Persist in prayer till your situation turns around for the better, being alert to what God instructs you.

Tip 9: Be a blessing to others. Give, including interceding for others.

PRAYERS FOR DIVINE PROTECTION AND PROVISION

These are warfare prayers.

Worship and praise God for at least 10 minutes (here you can prostrate yourself before God, kneel, or praise Him with dancing).

Then rise on your feet (or sit if tired) and read out loud the scripture below (if possible).

Psalm 91 NKJV

He who dwells in the secret place of the Most High, shall abide under the shadow of the Almighty.

I will say of the Lord, "He is my refuge and my fortress; my God, in Him I will trust."

Surely He shall deliver you from the snare of the fowler, and from the perilous pestilence.

He shall cover you with His feathers, and under His wings you shall take refuge; His truth shall be your shield and buckler.

You shall not be afraid of the terror by night, nor of the arrow that flies by day,

Nor of the pestilence that walks in darkness, nor of the destruction that lays waste at noonday.

A thousand may fall at your side, and ten thousand at your right hand; But it shall not come near you.

Only with your eyes shall you look, and see the reward of the wicked.

Because you have made the Lord, who is my refuge, even the Most High, your dwelling place,

No evil shall befall you, nor shall any plague come near your dwelling;

For He shall give His angels charge over you, to keep you in all your ways.

In their hands they shall bear you up, lest you dash your foot against a stone.

You shall tread upon the lion and the cobra, the young lion and the serpent you shall trample underfoot.

"Because he has set his love upon Me, therefore I will deliver him; I will set him on high, because he has known My name.

He shall call upon Me, and I will answer him; I will be with him in trouble; I will deliver him and honor him.

With long life I will satisfy him, and show him

My salvation."

Matthew 7:7-11 NKJV

"Ask, and it will be given to you; seek, and you will find; knock, and it will be opened to you. For everyone who asks receives, and he who seeks finds, and to him who knocks it will be opened. Or what man is there among you who, if his son asks for bread, will give him a stone? Or if he asks for a fish, will he give him a serpent? If you then, being evil, know how to give good gifts to your children, how much more will your Father who is in heaven give good things to those who ask Him!

Then move on to the prayer points below, pray them fervently, taking each prayer for at least 1 minute.

1) Lord, please grant me the grace to always do your will in Jesus' name (Matthew 7:21).

2) O Lord my God, grant me a heart that would fear You and always keep Your commandments in Jesus' name.

3) O Lord, make a hedge around me, around my household, and around all that I have on every side in Jesus' name (Job 1:10).

4) Lord bless the work of my hands and increase my possessions in the land in Jesus' name (Job 1:10).

5) I desire Your secret place, Lord, let me abide under Your shadow in the name of Jesus.

6) In Your mercy Lord, deliver ... [pick relevant aspects from the underlisted] from the snare of the fowler in Jesus' name

  - Me
  - My family
  - My marriage
  - My children
  - My career
  - My job
  - My business
  - My finances
  - My investments.

7) It is written, "You shall not be afraid of the terror by night, nor of the arrow that flies by day", I declare that as from today,

  - Terror attacks shall be far from me and my family in Jesus' name

- Accidents shall be far from me and my family in Jesus' name
- Injustice shall be far from me and my family in Jesus' name
- Untimely death shall be far from me and my family in Jesus' name
- Strife shall be far from me and my family in Jesus' name
- Oppression and abuse shall be far from me and my family in Jesus' name
- [you may add as the Holy Spirit leads you].

8) It is written, "A thousand may fall at your side, and ten thousand at your right hand; But it shall not come near you." I declare that it does not matter what the world is going through, the Lord shall perfect that which concerns me and my family. Therefore, economic hardships, strange diseases and plagues, and every arrow from the kingdom of darkness shall NOT be my portion in the mighty name of Jesus.

9) According to Your word O Lord, give your angels charge over me and my family in Jesus' name.

10) Lord, You tell me to ask for I shall

receive, to seek for I shall find, and to knock for it shall be opened unto me, therefore,

I ask that all the good works of my hands begin to prosper from now henceforth in Jesus' name

11) Let every good door that has closed unto me be opened in Jesus' name

12) Let every good opportunity I have lost in the past be restored unto me in Jesus' name

13) Let my health be released to flourish in Jesus' name

14) Let my finances be released to flourish in Jesus' name

15) Let my divine helpers be released to locate me speedily in Jesus' name.

16) According to Your promise Lord, satisfy me and my family with long life and show us Your salvation in Jesus' name.

17) Lord, I have called upon You, answer me in Your faithfulness in Jesus' name

Thank You, Lord, for answering my prayers.

Spend a moment to listen to the Lord. Then close the prayer session with high praises.

The End

Thank you for purchasing this book! Get your free copy of "Prayers for Healing and Business Success"
here:
https://bit.ly/nikeiza

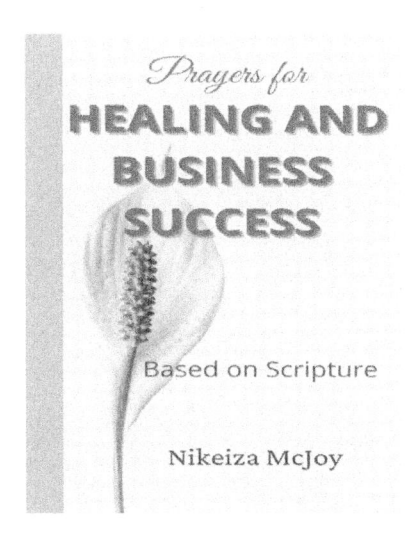

Please, Leave a Review

Would you mind taking a minute to leave your feedback? Reviews help me create better books and I will be very grateful.
Please, leave your review on Amazon.